GLUTEN-FREE
COOKBOOK

Tempting new ways to prepare all your favourite foods

Heather Whinney, Jane Lawrie & Fiona Hunter

CONTENTS

Guide to symbols

The recipes in this book are accompanied by symbols that alert you to important information.

 Tells you how many people the recipe serves, or how much is produced.

 Indicates how long you will need to prepare and cook a dish. Next to this symbol, it will also state if additional time is required for such things as marinating, standing, proving, or cooling.

 Alerts you to any special preparation or to parts of the recipe that take a long time.

 Denotes that special equipment is required.

 Accompanies freezing information.

 Shows whether a dish is relatively high (3 dots), medium (2 dots), or low (1 dot) in calories, saturated fat, and salt.

Eating well

Finding out you have a gluten intolerance can prompt mixed feelings. Relief that finally you're taking control of your health, but probably also concern that adopting a gluten-free diet might mean cutting out many of your favourite foods and accepting a less enjoyable, less flavourful diet. Yet nothing can be further from the truth and this book is here to prove you can eat fantastically well on a gluten-free diet.

DISCOVERING NEW FLAVOURS

Far from being a life sentence of disappointing food, cutting out gluten is a wonderful opportunity to explore new dishes made with grains and flours you may never have heard of before. Going gluten free is also the perfect excuse to release the home baker in you. A new generation of pre-blended flours, combined with the magic of xanthan gum, has transformed gluten-free baking, so that with our step-by-step instruction and specially created recipes you will still be able to enjoy all your favourite bakes.

Going gluten free is also about recovery. When first diagnosed, you are likely to be suffering the effects of poor nutrient absorption, which could include fatigue, joint pains, and various conditions related to vitamin and mineral deficiencies. By simply cutting out gluten your body will begin to recover, but it is also crucial to assess your diet to ensure it is properly balanced and that you're getting enough of the full range of nutrients. In the following pages, we outline the principles of a healthy, balanced diet and identify nutrients you should be eating more of. In the recipes, we have employed a nutrient boost icon to highlight particular health benefits, and each recipe features calorie and nutrient analysis so that you can plan a balanced, calorie-controlled diet.

EATING FOR HEALTH

We have selected a broad range of recipes to provide all the meal inspirations for healthy eating, but it should be emphasized that this is not a "diet" book of calorie-restricted recipes. Pies, cakes, pastries, and desserts are the dishes that people who give up gluten can miss the most, yet they tend to be high in calories. In creating gluten-free versions we have been guided by taste, not calorie counts, but just because they're gluten free doesn't mean you should be eating pies and cakes all the time! You'll find plenty of healthy recipes to choose for every day, and the guidelines will show you which dishes to enjoy as a rare treat

GUIDELINES per serving
- calories
- saturated fat
- salt

A balanced diet

Choosing a balanced diet is important for everyone and a gluten-free diet can be very healthy due to the emphasis placed on fresh and unprocessed foods. A balanced gluten-free diet should include plenty of fruit and vegetables, moderate amounts of lean protein, healthy unsaturated fats, wholegrain and unrefined gluten-free carbohydrates, and minimal amounts of saturated fats, salt, and sugar.

TACKLING NUTRIENT DEFICIENCY

Untreated coeliac disease can lead to nutritional deficiency in iron, calcium, magnesium, and zinc. When you start on a gluten free diet make sure it contains foods rich in these nutrients. Standard breakfast cereals and bread are often fortified with these nutrients, as well as B-group vitamins and fibre, but gluten-free versions are rarely fortified and alternative sources should be sought.

Iron
Needed for the manufacture of red blood cells. **Good GF sources** of iron include lean red meat, eggs, quinoa, dried fruit, lentils and chickpeas, baked beans, dark green leafy vegetables.

Calcium
Needed for strong bones, especially important for children, teenagers, and young adults. **Good GF sources** include yogurt, milk, cheese, canned fish eaten with their bones (e.g. sardines), almonds, sesame seeds, tofu.

Magnesium
Helps maintain muscle and nerve function, a healthy immune system, and strong bones. **Good GF sources** include nuts and seeds, beans and pulses, brown rice, dark green leafy vegetables.

Zinc
Essential for growth and development, a healthy immune system, and wound healing. **Good GF sources** include lean red meat, poultry, eggs, shellfish, beans, and nuts, especially Brazil nuts.

FOLATE
Involved in the production of red blood cells. Found in oranges, green vegetables, chickpeas, pulses.

IRON

Found in red meat, beans, and pulses
The body can more easily absorb iron
from non-meat sources if eaten in
conjunction with foods rich in vitamin C.

DIETARY FIBRE

Helps to keep the intestine healthy and
prevent constipation. Sources include
lentils, beans, pulses, quinoa,
buckwheat, brown rice, fruit, and veg.

B VITAMINS

Have many vital functions
Sources include potatoes,
broccoli, and bananas.

VITAMIN B12

B12 is important for a healthy
nervous system and is found in
fish, lean red meat, and eggs.

CALCIUM

Found in milk, yogurt, cheese, canned
sardines. Choose low- and reduced fat
dairy products when possible.

Baking bread

Home-made gluten-free bread is far superior to shop-bought. Using the right type of flour blend is key, as is the inclusion in the blend of xanthan gum, which enables the dough to rise. You can buy ready-mixed, gluten-free flour blends in many supermarkets and in health food stores.

CLASSIC WHITE LOAF

This moist, springy loaf slices brilliantly for sandwiches and makes great toast too. The bread will keep for 2–3 days wrapped in a plastic bag. Turn any leftovers into breadcrumbs and store in the freezer to use in stuffings, coatings for fried food, and so on. If you like, double the quantities and bake two loaves at the same time, then freeze one.

INGREDIENTS

oil for greasing
450g (1lb) gluten-free white bread
  flour, plus extra for dusting
2 tsp fast-action dried yeast
1 tsp salt
1 tbsp caster sugar
1 egg
2 tbsp vegetable oil
1 tsp vinegar
1 egg, beaten, for brushing

1 Lightly oil the tin. Sift together the flour, yeast, and salt into a large bowl, then stir in the sugar. Measure 300ml (10fl oz) lukewarm water into a jug, add the egg, oil, and vinegar and lightly whisk together with a fork.

2 Make a well in the centre of the dry ingredients and add the wet ingredients. Draw the flour into the liquid with a wooden spoon, mix well, and then bring together with your hands to form a dough.

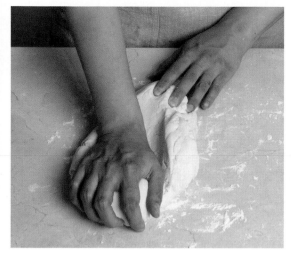

3 Turn the dough out onto a lightly floured surface and knead for about 5 minutes, or until smooth. To knead, hold the dough with one hand and stretch it with the palm of the other hand, then bring it back together, turn, and repeat.

4 Shape the dough into a rectangle roughly the size and shape of the tin and place it in the tin. Make 3 or 4 slashes on the top with a sharp knife. Cover loosely with oiled cling film and leave in a warm place to rise for 1 hour or until doubled.

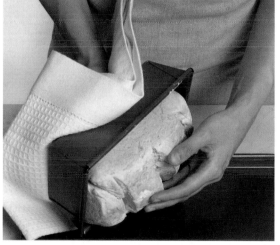

5 Preheat the oven to 220°C (425°F/Gas 7). Brush the top of the loaf with egg – this will help to colour it as gluten-free bread tends to bake to a paler colour than standard bread – and sprinkle with a little flour.

6 Bake for 35 minutes or until the loaf is risen and golden brown on top. Remove from the tin, transfer to a baking tray, and bake for a further 10 minutes to crisp the crust. Remove from the oven and leave to cool on a wire rack.

makes 1 loaf

prep 20 mins, plus rising • cook 25 mins

3 months

450g (1lb) loaf tin

Making pastry

Though a little more delicate to handle than traditional pastry, with practice you will soon master the art of gluten-free pastry and the results are well worth the effort. The addition of egg and xanthan gum helps the dough to bind, making it easier to roll out and giving the cooked pastry a crisp, flaky consistency that is almost indistinguishable from pastry made with wheat flour.

SHORTCRUST PASTRY

The pastry dough is here used to "blind" bake a case for tarts and quiches, but it is also perfect for making single and double crust pies and tartes Tatin. If you get a few cracks and holes as you lift the pastry and line the tin, simply patch them up with excess pastry and "glue" together with a little water to seal.

INGREDIENTS

225g (8oz) gluten-free plain flour,
   plus extra for dusting
1 tsp xanthan gum
pinch of salt
100g (3½oz) cold butter, cubed
1 egg, beaten

1 Preheat the oven to 200°C (400°F/Gas 6). Sift the flour, xanthan, and salt into a bowl and mix. Add the butter and rub it in with your fingertips until the mixture forms crumbs. You can also do this by pulsing the mixture in a food processor.

2 Add the egg and mix it in with a palette knife or round-bladed table knife. Gradually add 1–2 tablespoons cold water, a few drops at a time, mixing after each addition. Keep adding water and mixing until it just comes together to form a dough.

3 Transfer the dough to a floured surface and lightly knead until smooth. Wrap in cling film and chill in the fridge for 10 minutes. Roll out the pastry on a lightly floured surface until it is about 5mm (¼in) thick and large enough to fill the tin.

4 Carefully wrap the pastry around the rolling pin, lift over the tin, and unroll the pastry. Gently press the pastry into the base and sides of the tin. Trim the edges, repair any holes, and prick the base with a fork.

5 Line the pastry with baking parchment and weigh down the parchment with ceramic baking beans (or you can use dried beans, such as haricots). Place on a baking sheet and bake in the preheated oven for 15 minutes.

6 Remove the tart from the oven and carefully lift out the parchment and beans. Return to the oven for another 5 minutes to crisp up, then add the filling of your choice and bake as per recipe instructions.

makes 400g (14oz) enough for a medium tart case

prep 20 mins • cook 20 mins plus chilling

23cm (9in) round tart tin, ceramic baking beans (optional, see step 5)

Porridge with fruit compote

Classic porridge, served with aniseed-infused fruits, is a real treat for breakfast. For a less indulgent porridge, replace the cream with more milk.

INGREDIENTS

200g (7oz) rolled oats
750ml (1¼ pints) milk,
  plus extra if needed
250ml (9fl oz) single cream

For the compote

200g (7oz) soft pitted prunes
75g (2½oz) sour cherries
300ml (10fl oz) fresh orange juice
1 star anise

METHOD

1 First prepare the compote. Place the prunes and cherries in a pan and pour over the orange juice, add the star anise, bring to the boil, then reduce the heat and simmer gently for 15 minutes. Set aside to steep.

2 Meanwhile, place the oats in a pan. Add two-thirds of the milk and stir well so it is all incorporated. Bring slowly to the boil, stirring continuously, until the milk has been absorbed by the oats. Gradually stir in the remaining milk and the cream, bring back to the boil, and simmer gently, stirring, for 10–15 minutes or until thick and creamy. Add more milk, if needed.

3 Drain the dried fruit, reserving the liquid, and remove the star anise. Ladle the porridge into deep bowls and top with the drained fruit and a little of the reserved juice.

Variations

Try flavouring the porridge with some warming cinnamon spice: add 1 cinnamon stick and 2 teaspoons ground cinnamon to the oats along with the milk. When it's ready, remove the stick and serve with a sprinkle of cinnamon and a swirl of cream. The spice gives the porridge a sweet flavour, so there is no need to add sugar. You can also swap the fruits with dried apricots and sultanas, or figs and cranberries.

serves 6

prep 10 mins
• cook 20 mins

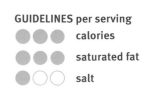

GUIDELINES per serving

calories

saturated fat

salt

Buckwheat pancakes with orange

The slightly nutty flavour of buckwheat flour combines well with oranges. The secret is to treat the batter gently.

INGREDIENTS

100g (3½oz) buckwheat flour
25g (scant 1oz) rice flour
salt
1 tsp sugar
1 egg, beaten

200ml (7fl oz) milk
3 oranges, peeled and thinly sliced,
   any juice reserved
1½ tbsp maple syrup, plus extra
sunflower oil, for frying

METHOD

1 To make the batter, place the flours in a bowl along with a pinch of salt and the sugar and mix. Make a well in the middle and add the egg. Stir well. Mix the milk and 150ml (5fl oz) water in a jug and gradually pour it into the flour, whisking with a balloon whisk until the batter is smooth and no longer lumpy. Set aside for 30 minutes to rest or overnight in the fridge.

2 For the oranges, heat a griddle pan over a high heat until hot. Mix any reserved orange juice with the maple syrup and brush over the orange slices to coat both sides. Place a few slices at a time on the griddle pan and cook each side for 2 minutes until they take on a little colour. Set aside.

3 Stir the batter. Heat 1 tablespoon oil in a non-stick frying pan or a crêpe pan over a high heat until hot. Swirl it around the pan so it just coats, and tip most of it out into a jug (to reuse). Reduce the heat to low-medium and add a ladleful of batter. Tilt the pan so it spreads; the mixture will be thick so it won't cover the pan completely. Cook for 2 minutes or until the underside is pale golden, then flip it and cook for 2 more minutes. To serve, top with orange slices and a drizzle of maple syrup. Repeat to use up all the batter.

serves 4

prep 15 mins plus resting • cook 30 mins

1 month

griddle pan

GUIDELINES per serving

calories
saturated fat
salt

Eggs Benedict

If you prefer white muffins, use the gluten-free white bread flour and add two tablespoons caster sugar.

INGREDIENTS

450g (1lb) gluten-free brown bread flour, plus extra for dusting
2 tsp fast-action dried yeast
1 tsp xanthan gum
salt and freshly ground black pepper
300ml (10fl oz) milk

90g (3oz) unsalted butter, plus extra
2 tbsp black treacle
5 eggs, plus 2 egg yolks
3 tbsp white wine vinegar

METHOD

1 Sift the flour, yeast, xanthan, and a pinch of salt into a large bowl and stir to combine. Warm the milk to lukewarm, add 15g (½oz) butter, the treacle, and 1 egg, and whisk with a fork. Make a well in the centre of the dry ingredients, add the wet ingredients, and mix. Turn onto a lightly floured surface and knead for 5 minutes until smooth. Roll out the dough 2cm (¾in) thick and cut out 8 rounds. Transfer to a floured baking sheet, cover with oiled cling film, and leave somewhere warm for 1 hour until doubled.

2 Heat a large, heavy frying pan or flat griddle. Add the muffins, making sure they don't touch each other, and cook over a medium heat for 6–7 minutes or until the bases are golden. Turn over, place a baking sheet on top of the pan to intensify the heat, and cook for 7–8 minutes until golden.

3 To poach the eggs, place a frying pan over a low heat and add boiling water to a depth of 2.5cm (1in). Carefully break 4 eggs, one at a time, into the water and let them barely simmer for 1 minute. Remove from the heat and set aside for 10 minutes to finish poaching.

4 For the hollandaise sauce, simmer the vinegar in a small pan until reduced by half. Pour into a heatproof bowl with the egg yolks and place over a pan of gently simmering water. Melt 75g (2½oz) butter, gradually add it to the bowl, and whisk continuously with a balloon whisk until a smooth, thick sauce forms. Remove from the heat and season. Split and butter the muffins, top each half with an egg, and pour over the sauce.

serves 4

prep 20 mins plus rinsing • cook 35 mins

3 month

7.5cm (3in) round metal cutter, griddle pan

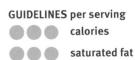
GUIDELINES per serving
calories
saturated fat
salt

Minestrone soup

This soup can use up a glut of seasonal vegetables, simply change them depending on the time of the year.

INGREDIENTS

1 ham knuckle or "hock"
1 tbsp olive oil
1 medium onion, finely chopped
2 bay leaves
3 large carrots, diced
1 fennel bulb, finely chopped
2 garlic cloves, finely chopped
freshly ground black pepper
4 large ripe tomatoes, chopped
leaves from a few thyme sprigs
pinch of freshly grated nutmeg

400g can chickpeas, drained
400g can cannellini or butter beans,
   drained and rinsed
100g (3½oz) broad beans, fresh
   or defrosted, shelled weight
100g (3½oz) peas, fresh or defrosted,
   shelled weight
200g (7oz) small gluten-free
   pasta shapes
100g (3½oz) spinach
grated Parmesan or Pecorino cheese

METHOD

1 Put the ham in a large pan and add enough cold water to nearly fill the pan. Bring to the boil, reduce to a medium-low heat, partially cover the pan with a lid, and cook for 1–1½ hours or until the ham begins to soften. Strain the stock, reserving the bones and meat. Strain the stock again, through a fine sieve, into a measuring jug; you will need 1.2 litres (2 pints), adding water if needed. Set aside. Strip the meat from the bones, discard the bones, and set the meat aside.

2 Heat the oil in a large, heavy pan. Add the onion and bay leaves, and cook over a medium-low heat for 5–7 minutes until soft. Add the carrots and fennel and cook for 8 more minutes until soft. Stir in the garlic and season with pepper, add the tomatoes, and cook on a low heat for 10 minutes. Ladle in a little stock if it starts to get dry. Add the thyme leaves, nutmeg, chickpeas, beans, and peas, and stir. Add enough stock to cover and simmer gently for 10 minutes. Add the pasta shapes, the reserved meat, and remaining stock. Bring to the boil, then simmer until the pasta is cooked. Add the spinach and stir. Taste and season again, if needed. Serve with the grated cheese.

serves 8

prep 40 mins
• cook 1 ¾ - 2¼ hours

3 months

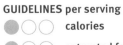

GUIDELINES per serving

calories

saturated fat

salt

16

Fennel soup with Parmesan thins

Parmesan thins are simplicity itself to make and elevate this rich, creamy soup to dinner party sophistication.

INGREDIENTS

1–2 tbsp olive oil
50g (1¾oz) butter
1 onion, finely chopped
salt and freshly ground black pepper
1 celery stick, finely chopped
1 carrot, finely chopped
2 garlic cloves, finely chopped

3–4 fennel bulbs, trimmed and finely chopped, fronds reserved to garnish
750ml (1¼ pints) hot gluten-free vegetable stock
4 tbsp finely grated Parmesan cheese
200ml (7fl oz) double cream
pinch of freshly grated nutmeg

METHOD

1 Heat 1 tablespoon oil and the butter in a large pan, add the onion, cook over a low heat for 5–6 minutes until soft, and season. Add the celery and carrot, and cook over a low heal for 10 minutes or until nicely golden. Add the garlic and fennel and cook over a very low heat for 5 minutes until the fennel begins to soften, adding more oil if needed. Pour over a little stock and bring to the boil. Add the remaining stock and bring to the boil again. Reduce to a simmer and cook for 20 minutes until the fennel is tender.

2 For the Parmesan thins, place 4 equal heaps of the grated Parmesan into a large, non-stick frying pan. Cook over a low heat and flatten each heap with the back of a spoon. Cook for a few minutes until the Parmesan begins to melt and forms a crust. Once it has started to crisp on the bottom and tiny bubbles start to appear around the edges, carefully flip each over using a palette knife. Cook for a further minute or so, then remove the pan from the heat, leaving the thins in the pan to keep warm.

3 Transfer the soup to a food processor and blend until smooth, then return to the pan, or use a stick blender. Season to taste, pour in the cream, and heat gently. Serve in wide bowls with a pinch of nutmeg and topped with a Parmesan thin. Garnish with the reserved fennel fronds.

serves 4

prep 20 mins
• cook 45 mins

food processor or stick blender

GUIDELINES per serving
●●○ calories
●●● saturated fat
●○○ salt

Beetroot and ginger soup

Earthy beetroot always makes a colourful soup. Here, ginger adds a pleasant zing and the wasabi cream, swirled in at the last minute, gives a fiery kick.

INGREDIENTS

500g (1lb 2oz) raw beetroot,
  stalks removed
salt
pinch of sugar
1 tbsp olive oil
bunch of spring onions, trimmed
  and finely chopped
5cm (2in) piece of fresh root
  ginger, peeled and grated

salt and freshly ground black pepper
750ml (1¼ pints) hot gluten-free
  vegetable stock
3 tbsp soured cream
¼ tsp wasabi paste, or more
  if you like it hot

METHOD

1 To cook the beetroot, place them in a pan of salted water, add the sugar, and bring to the boil. Cook on a low-medium heat with the lid ajar for 40 minutes or until the beetroot is tender when poked with a sharp knife. Drain and, when cool enough to handle, peel and roughly chop the beetroot.

2 In a clean pan, heat the oil and add the spring onions. Cook for 2–3 minutes on a medium heat, just enough for them to soften, then add the ginger and cook for a further minute. Add the chopped beetroot and stir well to coat with the oil. Season, pour in the stock, and bring to the boil.

3 Reduce to a simmer and cook gently for about 10 minutes, then ladle into a food processor and blend until smooth, or use a stick blender. Taste and season some more, if needed. Mix the soured cream with the wasabi. Ladle the soup into bowls with a swirl of the wasabi cream.

serves 4

prep 10 mins
• cook 55 mins

food processor
or stick blender

GUIDELINES per serving

calories

saturated fat

salt

Vegetable tempura

Don't let the batter for these Japanese snacks sit: it needs to be used immediately, so prepare the vegetables ahead.

INGREDIENTS

1 red pepper, deseeded and
  cut into strips
1 small head of broccoli, broken
  into florets
1 medium onion, cut into eighths
2 carrots, cut into batons
1 tbsp cornflour
sunflower oil, for frying

For the dipping sauce

2 tbsp gluten-free mirin
3 tbsp tamari (gluten-free soy sauce)

1–2 tsp sugar, or to taste
1 tbsp lime juice

For the batter

1 egg yolk
120ml (4fl oz) sparkling mineral
  water, ice cold
100g (3½oz) rice flour, sieved
salt and freshly ground black pepper

METHOD

1 To make the sauce, place the mirin, tamari, and sugar in a bowl and mix. Then add the lime juice and 3 tablespoons water to dilute it. Mix again, taste, and add more water if needed. Set aside. For the batter, place the egg yolk in a bowl and mix with a fork. Pour in the mineral water and mix. Add the rice flour and seasoning and mix lightly.

2 Toss the prepared vegetables in the cornflour. Pour the oil into a wok, to a depth of 7.5cm (3in). Heat on high until hot. Don't leave the wok or pan unattended, take off the heat when not using, and keep a fire blanket nearby in case of fire. Dip the vegetables, one by one, into the batter until just coated, then place them in the oil. Don't overcrowd the pan. Remove with a slotted spoon as soon as the batter is crispy and golden, about 2–3 minutes, and drain on kitchen paper. Continue with the rest of the vegetables and batter. Serve hot with the dipping sauce.

serves 6

prep 25 mins
• cook 10 mins

wok or large, deep,
non-stick frying pan

GUIDELINES per serving
calories
saturated fat
salt

Crab cakes with sweet and sour sauce

Succulent bites of minced crab flavoured with chilli and coriander make a perfect culinary treat.

INGREDIENTS

400g (14oz) fresh or canned
  crab meat
1 bunch of spring onions, trimmed
  and finely chopped
handful of fresh coriander,
  roughly chopped
1 chilli, deseeded and finely chopped
1 egg, lightly beaten
1–2 tbsp rice flour, for dusting
sunflower oil, for frying

For the sweet and sour sauce

5 tbsp rice vinegar
2 tsp cornflour
150ml (5fl oz) pineapple juice
2 tbsp passata
1–2 tsp sugar, or more to taste
salt and freshly ground black pepper

METHOD

1 First make the sauce. Place all the ingredients in a small pan and gently bring to the boil, stirring well as you go. Reduce to a simmer and cook for 10 minutes, until thickened. Season to taste, then set aside.

2 For the crab cakes, place the crab meat, spring onion, coriander, and chilli in a food processor and pulse until well minced. Season and pulse again. Spoon the mixture into a bowl and mix in the egg, a little at a time. Keep adding until the mixture is soft and pliable but not too mushy; it is best to mix with your hands.

3 Lightly flour your hands, scoop out balls of the mixture, and flatten them into about 16 mini rounds. Place them on a baking sheet lined with baking parchment and chill in the fridge for 30 minutes to firm up.

4 Heat a little oil in a non-stick frying pan and add the cakes a few at a time. Cook on each side until golden, about 5–6 minutes in total. Place on kitchen paper to drain, then serve with the sweet and sour sauce.

serves 4

prep 15 mins plus chilling • cook 30 mins

3 months crab cakes only

food processor

GUIDELINES per serving
calories
saturated fat
salt

Quiche Lorraine

A timeless classic that never fails to please. You can add fresh chopped tomatoes into the mix, but do keep this tart simple.

INGREDIENTS

400g (14oz) gluten-free
  shortcrust pastry (see p10)
gluten-free plain flour, for dusting

For the filling

1 tbsp olive oil
1 onion, finely chopped

salt and freshly ground black pepper
200g (7oz) bacon or pancetta, cubed
200g (7oz) Cheddar cheese, grated
250ml (9fl oz) double cream
3 eggs, lightly beaten
50g (1¾oz) Gruyère cheese, grated

METHOD

1 Preheat the oven to 200°C (400°F/Gas 6). Roll out the pastry on a lightly floured surface to a thickness of 5mm (¼in). Line the tin with the pastry, patching up any holes, then neaten and trim the edges. Prick the base with a fork, line with baking parchment and fill with baking beans, then bake in the oven for 15 minutes. Remove the beans and paper and return to the oven for another 5 minutes to crisp up. Set aside. Reduce the oven temperature to 180°C (350°F/Gas 4).

2 Meanwhile, heat the oil in a frying pan, add the onion, and cook for 6–8 minutes or until beginning to soften. Season to taste with salt and pepper, then transfer to a bowl and set aside to cool. Add the bacon or pancetta to the pan and cook on a medium heat for 5–8 minutes until golden. Set aside.

3 Sprinkle the onion over the base of the pastry case. Add the bacon or pancetta, draining off any excess fat, then add the Cheddar, mixing it up a little. Mix the cream and eggs together and season. Pour the mixture into the case and sprinkle over the Gruyère cheese. Cook for 25–30 minutes until the top is dark golden and the quiche is set. Leave to cool slightly in the tin to set more, then serve warm.

serves 6

prep 20 mins
• cook 1 hour

20.5cm (8in) round, loose bottomed tart tin, at least 4.5cm (1¾in) deep

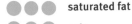

GUIDELINES per serving

calories

saturated fat

salt

Mushroom burgers

Served with miso-roasted chips and tahini dip, these burgers have lots of gutsy flavours. Make mini ones for the kids.

INGREDIENTS

3 tbsp olive oil
1 onion, finely chopped
500g (1lb 2oz) chestnut mushrooms,
   pulsed in a food processor
4 anchovies, finely chopped
tamari (gluten-free soy sauce)
125g (4½oz) gluten-free breadcrumbs
1 egg, lightly beaten
salt and freshly ground black pepper

For the miso chips

4 sweet potatoes, peeled and
   cut into thin chips
1 tbsp olive oil
1 tbsp sweet miso or tamari

For the tahini dip

2 garlic cloves, grated
pinch of sea salt
3 tbsp tahini
juice of 1 lemon

METHOD

1 Preheat the oven to 200°C (400°F/Gas 6). Heat 1 tablespoon oil in a large frying pan, add the onion, and cook on a low heat for 3–4 minutes. Add the mushrooms and cook for 6 minutes or until they start to release their juices. Stir through the anchovies and tamari and cook for 1 minute. Transfer to a large bowl. Add the breadcrumbs and trickle in the egg until the mixture binds well. Add more crumbs if it's too wet and season well. Make 4 large balls from the mixture and form into burgers. Sit them on a baking sheet lined with baking parchment and chill in the fridge for 30 minutes.

2 For the chips, toss the potatoes with the oil and miso or tamari, and spread out in a roasting tin. Roast in the oven for 20 minutes until the chips begin to turn golden and are crisp. For the tahini dip, grind the garlic and sea salt in a pestle and mortar. Add the tahini and mix. Add about 2 tablespoons water to loosen it. Stir through the lemon juice.

3 To cook the burgers, heat half the remaining oil in a large frying pan on a medium heat, add the burgers 2 at a time, and cook for 3–5 minutes on each side, until golden. Repeat to cook the remaining burgers. Serve with the sweet potato chips and tahini dip.

serves 4

prep 20 mins plus chilling
• cook 50 mins

food processor

GUIDELINES per serving
●●○ calories
●○○ saturated fat
●●● salt

Stuffed butternut squash

A vibrantly coloured autumnal dish that would work just as well with pumpkin. You could use Cheddar, Parmesan, or goat's cheese instead of the Gruyère.

INGREDIENTS

2 medium, or 4 small, butternut squash, halved lengthways and deseeded
1 tbsp olive oil, plus extra for greasing
225g (8oz) Gruyère cheese, grated

For the fruit and nut mix

100g (3½oz) hazelnuts, toasted and roughly chopped

75g (2½oz) dried cranberries, roughly chopped
small handful of flat-leaf parsley, finely chopped
pinch of dried chilli flakes
salt and freshly ground black pepper
wild rocket salad, to serve

METHOD

1 Preheat the oven to 190°C (375°F/Gas 5). Brush 2 baking sheets with oil. With a sharp knife, score a crisscross pattern on the flesh of each butternut squash half and brush with the oil. Sit the squash on a greased baking sheet, flesh-side down, and roast for about 1 hour until the flesh begins to soften. Now scoop out most of the flesh, leaving a thin layer still attached to the skins, and reserve the hollowed squash halves.

2 Place the flesh in a bowl and mash with a fork. Add all the fruit and nut mix ingredients to the mashed squash and mix well. Divide the mixture between the squash skins.

3 Sprinkle over the cheese and return the squash halves to the oven. Bake for a further 10–15 minutes until the cheese is bubbling. Serve the squash with a lightly dressed wild rocket salad.

serves 4

prep 15 mins
• cook 1¼ hours

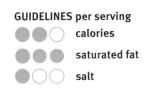

GUIDELINES per serving

calories

saturated fat

salt

Pasta Genovese

A quick home-made pesto is tossed with linguine for this timeless classic from the Italian city of Genoa.

INGREDIENTS

2 garlic cloves, roughly chopped
large handful of basil leaves
100g (3½oz) Parmesan cheese,
    finely grated
100g (3½oz) Pecorino cheese,
    finely grated
85g (3oz) pine nuts, toasted
salt and freshly ground black pepper
about 200ml (7fl oz) extra
    virgin olive oil
350g (12oz) gluten-free linguine
tomato salad, to serve

METHOD

1 To prepare the pesto, place the garlic in a food processor and whizz until minced. Then add the basil leaves, Parmesan, Pecorino, pine nuts, and seasoning, and pulse a few times until it reaches your preferred texture.
2 Slowly trickle in the olive oil, pressing the pulse button as you go, adding as much or little to get the correct consistency – avoid a sloppy pesto. Taste and season if required. Set aside. Alternatively, make the pesto in a pestle and mortar for a coarser texture.
3 Put the pasta in a large pan of boiling salted water and cook according to the packet instructions, giving it a stir at the beginning to prevent it from sticking together. Drain well and return to the pan with a little of the cooking water. Add enough pesto to just coat and toss well. Serve with a fresh tomato salad.

serves 4

prep 10 mins
• cook 12 mins

food processor

GUIDELINES per serving
calories
saturated fat
salt

Smoked salmon pasta

Cream cheese makes an instant and cheap pasta sauce for this easy mid-week supper dish.

INGREDIENTS

350g (12oz) gluten-free linguine or
   other pasta shapes
200g (7oz) cream cheese
250g (9oz) smoked salmon
   trimmings, chopped
2–3 sprigs of dill, finely chopped
salt and freshly ground black pepper
wild rocket leaves dressed with olive
   oil and lemon juice, to serve

METHOD

1 Put the pasta in a large pan of boiling salted water and cook according to the packet instructions. Give it a stir at the beginning of cooking to prevent it from sticking together. Drain and return to the pan with a little of the cooking water.
2 Stir the cream cheese through the pasta, so it melts to form a sauce. Add the salmon and stir again.
3 Sprinkle over the dill and season. Serve with a lightly dressed, lemony wild rocket salad.

serves 4

prep 10 mins
• cook 15 mins

GUIDELINES per serving

calories

saturated fat

salt

Mee goreng

This classic Malaysian dish is traditionally made with wheat egg noodles but works just as well with rice noodles.

INGREDIENTS

4 garlic cloves, roughly chopped

10 black peppercorns

1 red chilli, deseeded and
  roughly chopped

3 tbsp sunflower oil

225g (8oz) firm tofu, cut into
  cubes or strips

3 tbsp tamari (gluten-free soy sauce)

300ml (10fl oz) hot gluten-free
  vegetable stock

300g (10oz) dried vermicelli
  rice noodles

½ small, firm white cabbage,
  finely shredded

handful of beansprouts

4 spring onions, finely sliced

4 eggs, fried, to serve (optional)

METHOD

1 Grind the garlic, pepper, and chilli to a paste in a pestle and mortar, or put in a small food processor and whizz until minced. Heat the oil in a wok on a medium-high heat, add the garlic mixture, and cook for a few seconds. Add the tofu and cook for 5–8 minutes until it starts to turn golden. Add the tamari and stir carefully, then let it bubble for 2–3 minutes. Add the stock, bubble again, and cook until the mixture has reduced by half.

2 Meanwhile, sit the noodles in a bowl, cover with boiling water, and leave for 5 minutes until beginning to soften, then drain.

3 Add the cabbage to the mixture and mix quickly, then add the noodles and mix well. Add the beansprouts and spring onions, toss together, and remove from the heat. Serve hot, topped with a fried egg and more tamari, if needed.

serves 4

prep 25-30 mins
• cook 20 mins

wok or large deep,
non-stick frying pan
• food processor

GUIDELINES per serving

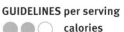 calories

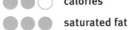 saturated fat

 salt

Salt-and-pepper beef noodles

Succulent strips of beef are stir-fried in a Chinese-style sauce with crisp mangetout.

INGREDIENTS

200g (7oz) dried rice noodles

600g (1lb 5oz) sirloin steak, thinly sliced

salt and freshly ground black pepper

1 tsp Sichuan pepper

1 tbsp sunflower oil

3 garlic cloves, finely sliced

5cm (2in) piece of fresh root ginger, peeled and finely sliced

1 green chilli, deseeded and sliced into fine strips

200g (7oz) mangetout or sugarsnap peas, sliced (optional)

3 spring onions, finely sliced, to garnish

For the sauce

2 tbsp tamari (gluten-free soy sauce)

1 tbsp gluten-free nam pla (fish sauce)

1 tbsp cornflour

1 tsp caster sugar

METHOD

1 Place the noodles in a bowl, cover with boiling water, and leave for 10 minutes or as per packet instructions. Drain and set aside.

2 For the sauce, mix together the tamari, nam pla, cornflour, and sugar and set aside.

3 Toss the beef with the salt and pepper and Sichuan pepper. Heat the oil in a wok, add the beef, and stir-fry on a medium-high heat for 3–4 minutes or until browned all over, then remove.

4 Add the garlic, ginger, chilli, and mangetout or sugarsnap peas (if using) to the wok, adding a little more oil if needed, and stir-fry for 2 minutes on a medium-high heat. Pour in the sauce and let it bubble. Add 2–3 tablespoons water – more if it is still too thick – and let it cook for another 2 minutes. Return the beef to the wok and stir to coat, then add the noodles and stir again. Spoon out into a serving dish and top with the spring onion.

serves 4

prep 15 mins
• cook 20 mins

wok or large deep, non-stick frying pan

GUIDELINES per serving

calories

saturated fat

salt

Spiced noodles with aromatic red snapper

Sambal oelek, an Indonesian hot chilli condiment, is the perfect partner for this delicate fish.

INGREDIENTS

1 red snapper, filleted, skinned, and
  chopped into large chunks
250g (9oz) dried fine rice noodles
1 tbsp sunflower oil
bunch of spring onions, sliced
300g (10oz) French beans, trimmed
  and chopped
1 red pepper, deseeded and
  finely chopped
2 garlic cloves, finely chopped
1–2 tsp sambal oelek, or 1 chopped
  red chilli

1 tbsp tamari (gluten-free soy sauce)
handful of fresh coriander, leaves only
1 orange, peeled and segmented

For the marinade

zest and juice of 1 orange
2 tsp finely chopped thyme leaves
1 red chilli, deseeded and finely chopped
2 garlic cloves, finely chopped
1 tbsp olive oil
salt and freshly ground black pepper

METHOD

1 Place the fish in a shallow dish. Combine all the marinade ingredients in a jug, stir well, and pour over the fish, turning the pieces to coat. Set aside to marinate for up to 1 hour. Preheat the oven to 180°C (350°F/Gas 4). Remove the fish using a slotted spoon and place in a roasting tin. Roast for 20–25 minutes or until the fish is cooked through and turning opaque. Set aside.

2 Cover the noodles with boiling water and leave for 10 minutes or as per packet instructions. Drain. Add oil to the wok or pan and swirl it around. Add the spring onions and cook on a medium-high heat for 2–3 minutes until soft. Add the beans and stir. Cook for 5 minutes until they begin to soften. Stir in the pepper and garlic and cook for 2–3 minutes.

3 Add sambal oelek or chilli and tamari. Add the noodles and toss. Cook for 3–5 minutes and transfer to a serving dish. Top with the fish and coriander. Serve with orange segments.

serves 4

**prep 15 mins plus marinating
• cook 25-30 mins**

**wok or large deep,
non-stick frying pan**

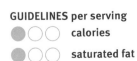

GUIDELINES per serving
○○○ calories
○○○ saturated fat
○○○ salt

Haddock and turmeric rice

Children will love this kedgeree-style dish, just go easy on the garam masala – a pinch will suffice.

INGREDIENTS

300g (10oz) basmati rice
salt and freshly ground black pepper
350g (12oz) undyed smoked
   haddock fillet
300ml (10fl oz) milk
1 tbsp olive oil
knob of butter
1 onion, finely chopped
2 tsp turmeric

2 tsp garam masala or mild
   curry powder
75g (2½oz) frozen peas, defrosted
4 eggs, hard boiled and halved
fresh coriander or flat-leaf parsley
   leaves, roughly chopped,
lemon wedges, and mango
   chutney, to serve

METHOD

1 Put the rice in a large pan and pour in enough water to cover. Season with salt and simmer gently with the lid ajar for 10–15 minutes until tender and cooked. Drain and set aside.

2 Lay the fish in a frying pan, skin-side down, and cover with milk or 300ml (10fl oz) water. Cover the pan and cook on a low heat for 4–5 minutes until the fish just begins to flake. Remove with a slotted spoon, discard the skin, and set aside, keeping warm.

3 Heat the oil and butter in a large frying pan and add the onion. Cook on a low heat for 2–3 minutes. Season to taste. Stir in the turmeric and garam masala and cook for 1–2 minutes. Stir in the rice and add the peas. On a very low heat, stir to combine and warm the peas through, then flake the fish into chunky pieces and add to the pan. Top with the eggs and season to taste. Sprinkle over the coriander or parsley and add a squeeze of lemon. Serve with mango chutney on the side.

serves 4

prep 20 mins
• cook 25 mins

GUIDELINES per serving

● ● ○ calories
● ● ● ○ saturated fat
● ● ○ salt

Beer-battered fish and chips

A favourite classic – the batter serves as a protective casing while the fish cooks, leaving it flaky and delicate.

INGREDIENTS

800g (1¾lb) potatoes, peeled and cut into thickish fingers
3 tbsp olive oil
pinch of sea salt
4 haddock or cod fillets, skin on
salt and freshly ground black pepper
juice of ½ lemon

225g (8oz) gluten-free self-raising flour, sifted, plus extra for dusting
300ml (10fl oz) gluten-free beer
vegetable oil, for frying
lemon wedges, to serve

METHOD

1 For the chips, preheat the oven to 200°C (400°F/Gas 6). Tip the potatoes into a large roasting tin, add the olive oil, and coat them well. Spread them out so they roast rather than steam, and sprinkle with sea salt. Cook in the oven for 30–40 minutes until golden, turning them halfway through cooking.

2 Meanwhile, season the fish, squeeze a little lemon juice over each fillet, and dust with a little flour. Place the remaining flour along with a pinch of salt to a bowl and slowly pour in the beer, whisking as you go. You may not need all the beer, as the mixture should be thick. If it is too runny, it won't stick to the fish, so stop when you reach the required consistency.

3 Fill a deep-fat fryer with the vegetable oil, or pour it into a large pan so that it is one-third full, and heat to 190°C (375°F); maintain this temperature throughout. Do not leave the pan or fryer unattended, switch off when not using, and keep a fire blanket nearby in case of fire. Hold the fish by the tail and pass it through the batter so that it's completely coated, then add it to the oil. Cook 2 fillets at a time for 2–3 minutes, turn over, and cook for a further 2–3 minutes until crisp and golden. Transfer to kitchen paper to drain and repeat with the remaining fish, keeping the finished pieces warm in a low oven. Serve with the chips and lemon wedges.

serves 4

prep 15 mins
• cook 40 mins

deep fat fryer
(optional)

GUIDELINES per serving
●●○ calories
●○○ saturated fat
●○○ salt

Chicken tikka masala

A takeaway favourite, the marinade gives this home-made version quite a kick that's softened by the creamy sauce.

INGREDIENTS

4 chicken breasts, skinless, cut into
  2.5cm (1in) cubes

For the marinade

4 tbsp natural yogurt
juice of ½ lemon
2 tsp ground cumin
1 tsp ground cinnamon
1–2 tsp cayenne pepper
2 tsp freshly ground black pepper
5cm (2in) piece of fresh root ginger,
  peeled and grated
pinch of salt

For the sauce

25g (scant 1oz) butter
1 onion, finely chopped
2 garlic cloves, grated
1 red chilli, deseeded and
  finely chopped
1 tsp ground cumin
2 tsp paprika
400ml (14fl oz) passata
150ml (5fl oz) double cream
salt and freshly ground black pepper
handful of fresh coriander leaves,
  roughly chopped
rice, to serve

METHOD

1 Mix all the ingredients for the marinade and transfer to a rectangular dish. Thread the chicken onto the skewers, sit them in the dish, and cover with the marinade. Then cover the dish and marinate in the fridge for 2 hours.

2 For the sauce, melt the butter in a medium pan, add the onion, and cook over a medium heat for 2–3 minutes or until soft. Add the garlic and chilli and cook for 2 minutes. Stir in the cumin and paprika, then add the passata and the cream and simmer on a gentle heat for 20–25 minutes until it thickens. Season, add half the coriander, and stir well.

3 Remove the skewers from the marinade and cook under a medium grill for 15–20 minutes until golden brown. Remove the chicken, add to the sauce, and cook for a further 2 minutes. Garnish with the remaining coriander and serve with rice.

serves 4

prep 15 mins plus
marinating • cook 50 mins

4 skewers; if wooden, soak
for 30 mins before use

GUIDELINES per serving
calories
saturated fat
salt

Roast chicken with orange and tamari

A simple sweet-and-spicy dish. Chicken drumsticks and wings would also work well.

INGREDIENTS

8 chicken thighs on the bone
½ tsp ground ginger
1 tsp ground dried mint
¼ tsp ground allspice
salt and freshly ground black pepper
2 tbsp pomegranate seeds
handful of fresh coriander leaves,
  roughly chopped

steamed rice or baby roast
  potatoes, to serve

For the marinade

3 tbsp tamari (gluten-free soy sauce)
juice of 3 oranges or 4 tangerines

METHOD

1 Mix together the marinade ingredients in a large bowl, then add the chicken pieces and stir to coat thoroughly. Cover and put in the fridge for 30 minutes or 2 hours if time permits.

2 Preheat the oven to 200°C (400°F/Gas 6). Mix together the ginger, mint, and allspice. Place the chicken pieces and marinade in a roasting tin, sprinkle over the spice mixture, season, and bake in the oven for 40 minutes until golden.

3 Remove from the oven, transfer to a serving plate, and sprinkle over the pomegranate seeds and coriander. Serve the chicken with steamed rice or baby roast potatoes.

serves 4

prep 15 mins plus
marinating • cook 40 mins

GUIDELINES per serving
calories
saturated fat
salt

Beef and beer casserole

A really hearty dish with slow-cooked beef simmered in a light beer. Perfect comfort food.

INGREDIENTS

1 tbsp rice flour
salt and freshly ground black pepper
1kg (2¼lb) braising steak, chuck, or
  skirt, cut into large bite-sized pieces
3 tbsp olive oil
300g (10oz) carrots, cut into chunks
1 celeriac, peeled and cut into chunks
3 leeks, trimmed and cut into chunks
300ml (10fl oz) gluten-free beer
750ml (1¼ pints) hot gluten-free
  vegetable stock
50g (1¾oz) quinoa

For the herb dumplings

½ onion, finely chopped
½ tbsp olive oil
small handful of flat-leaf parsley, finely chopped
a few rosemary leaves, finely chopped
75g (2½oz) gluten-free breadcrumbs
1 tsp gluten-free ready-grated horseradish
1 tsp Dijon mustard
1 egg

METHOD

1 Preheat the oven to 160°C (325°F/Gas 3). Season the flour and toss with the beef to coat. Heat 2 tablespoons of oil in the casserole and brown the beef in batches over a medium heat for 5 minutes per batch, until sealed. Set aside.

2 Add the remaining oil to the casserole and cook the vegetables for 5–6 minutes, until golden. Pour in a little of the beer, raise the heat, and stir to scrape up any bits from the bottom of the casserole. Add the remaining beer and simmer on a medium heat for 5 minutes. Pour in the stock, bring to the boil, reduce to a simmer, return the meat to the casserole along with the quinoa. Season, cover, and cook in the oven for 1½ hours before adding the dumplings; top up with hot water if it looks dry.

3 For the dumplings, cook the onion in the oil in over a medium heat until soft. Add the remaining ingredients, season, and stir until mixture comes together. Form 12 dumpling balls and set aside. When ready, remove the casserole from the oven and add the dumplings, pushing them down into the sauce. Re-cover the casserole and return to the oven for 30 minutes, removing the lid for the last 5 minutes.

serves 6

prep 40 mins
• cook 2 hours

large flameproof casserole
or lidded ovenproof pan

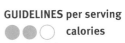

GUIDELINES per serving
calories
saturated fat
salt

Cassoulet

This intensely rich French stew is well worth the wait and lovely to cook on a cold winter's day.

INGREDIENTS

4 duck legs

3 tbsp olive oil

salt and freshly ground black pepper

1kg (2¼lb) rindless belly pork, cut into bite-sized pieces

6 gluten-free Toulouse sausages, each cut into 4

3 carrots, sliced

2 onions, finely sliced

4 garlic cloves, finely chopped

4 tomatoes, skinned and finely chopped

2 x 400g cans haricot beans, drained and rinsed

1 bouquet garni

300–400ml (10–14fl oz) hot gluten-free chicken stock

handful of gluten-free breadcrumbs

Savoy cabbage or green beans, to serve

METHOD

1 Preheat the oven to 220°C (425°F/Gas 7). Rub the duck legs with 1 tablespoon oil and then sprinkle and rub all over with salt. Put in a roasting tin and bake in the oven for 15–20 minutes until brown and crisp. Remove and set aside. Reduce the oven temperature to 170°C (340°F/Gas 3½).

2 In the large flameproof casserole, heat the remaining oil on a medium heat, add the pork and cook, stirring frequently, until it begins to brown. Add the sausages and cook for 4–5 minutes, then add the carrots and cook for 5 minutes. Add the onions and cook for 2 minutes. Stir in the garlic, cook for 1 minute, then add the tomatoes, beans, and bouquet garni and season well.

3 Add 300ml (10fl oz) stock to the pan; check as it cooks and add more stock if the cassoulet looks like it's drying out. Cover and cook in the oven for 1 hour, then add the duck legs, combine well, leave uncovered, and cook for a further 1 hour. Sprinkle over the breadcrumbs for the last 30 minutes of cooking; cover loosely with foil if it begins to brown too much. Stir occasionally. When ready, remove the bouquet garni and serve piping hot with Savoy cabbage or green beans.

serves 6

prep 15 mins
• cook 2½ hours

large flameproof casserole
or lidded oveproof pan

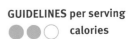

GUIDELINES per serving

calories

saturated fat

salt

Lamb and beans simmered in wine

An easy one-pan dish that can be served straight to the table with some gluten-free bread and steamed greens.

INGREDIENTS

2 tbsp olive oil
1 red onion, finely chopped
500g (1lb 2oz) lamb leg steaks, trimmed of fat and cut into bite-sized pieces
salt and freshly ground black pepper
pinch of dried chilli flakes
pinch of dried oregano
1 tbsp gluten-free plain flour
3 garlic cloves, finely sliced

150ml (5fl oz) dry white wine
300ml (10fl oz) hot gluten-free vegetable stock
400g can cannellini beans, drained and rinsed
400g can flageolet beans, drained and rinsed
lemon wedges, steamed greens, and gluten-free crusty bread, to serve

METHOD

1 Heat half the oil in a large, heavy frying pan, add the onion, and cook on a low heat for 5 minutes, then remove the onion and set aside. Add the remaining oil to the pan. Season the lamb with salt and pepper, the chilli flakes, and the oregano, then toss in the flour and add to the pan.

2 Cook on a medium-high heat for 10–15 minutes until golden on all sides, then return the onion to the pan, add the garlic, and cook for 2 minutes. Increase the heat, add the wine, and bubble for a minute. Add the stock and bubble for 1 more minute.

3 Reduce to a simmer and stir the beans into the mixture. Cover with a lid, leaving it slightly ajar, and cook gently for 30–40 minutes; make sure it doesn't dry out and top up with stock or hot water if needed. Season to taste and serve with lemon wedges, steamed greens, and crusty bread.

serves 4

prep 10 mins
• cook 1 hour

GUIDELINES per serving
●○○○ calories
●●○○ saturated fat
●○○○ salt

Pork enchiladas

A rich mix of fabulous flavours: tortillas filled with smoky pork and tomato salsa, baked with cheese and cream.

INGREDIENTS

350g (12oz) pork tenderloin
6 gluten-free corn tortillas
6 tbsp soured cream, to top
75g (2½oz) mature Cheddar
   cheese, grated, to top

For the marinade

2 tbsp olive oil
1 chipotle chilli, finely chopped,
   or dried jalapeño chilli, or 1 tbsp
   adobo sauce, or a generous splash
   of smoked chipotle Tabasco sauce
2 tsp coriander seeds

pinch of ground cinnamon
salt and freshly ground black pepper
pinch of sugar

For the tomato salsa

500g (1lb 2oz) vine-ripened tomatoes
1 red chilli, halved and deseeded
1 tbsp olive oil
2 spring onions, finely chopped
juice of 1 lime
salt and freshly ground black pepper
handful of fresh coriander leaves,
   finely chopped

METHOD

1 Put the pork in a shallow dish, mix the marinade ingredients, and pour over the pork to cover. Leave for 20 minutes or longer if time permits. Preheat the oven to 200°C (400°F/ Gas 6). Transfer the pork (with the marinade) to a roasting tin and cook for 40 minutes, basting occasionally so the pork doesn't dry out. Remove and set aside.

2 For the salsa, heat a griddle pan to hot. Toss the tomatoes and chilli with the oil and add to the pan. Cook over a medium-high heat for 5–6 minutes, turning halfway, until lightly charred. Remove and pulse with the spring onions and lime juice in a food processor until chopped. Season to taste, transfer to a bowl, and stir through the coriander.

3 Shred the pork, retaining any of the juices. Lay out the tortillas and spoon the pork into the centre of each. Spoon over the salsa and roll up the tortillas. Sit them in an ovenproof dish, spoon the soured cream on top, and sprinkle the cheese. Bake for 15–20 minutes until the cheese has melted. Serve with the remaining salsa and a splash of Tabasco sauce, if liked.

serves 4

prep 20-25 mins
plus marinating
• cook 1 hour

griddle pan
• food processor

GUIDELINES per serving

calories

saturated fat

salt

Toad in the hole

If making for kids, halve the sausages and stand them on end in the tin so they stick up, and omit the wine in the gravy.

INGREDIENTS

2 tbsp olive oil
8 gluten-free sausages, pork or beef
125g (4½oz) gluten-free plain flour
pinch of salt
2 eggs
300ml (10fl oz) milk
1 tbsp Dijon mustard (optional)

For the gravy

100ml (3½fl oz) red wine
1 tbsp cornflour
300ml (10fl oz) hot gluten-free
  pork or beef stock
salt and freshly ground black pepper
few sprigs of rosemary

METHOD

1 Preheat the oven to 220°C (425°F/Gas 7). Heat half the oil in a large frying pan, add the sausages, and cook on a medium-high heat for 10–15 minutes, until golden all over. Remove, put them in a baking tin, and set aside.

2 For the batter, place the flour and salt in a bowl. Make a well in the centre, add the eggs and a little milk, and stir, bringing in a little flour. Slowly add the milk and continue stirring, pulling in more flour from the edges until you have a smooth batter. Use a balloon whisk at the end to avoid lumps. Stir in the mustard (if using). Add the remaining oil to the baking tin with the sausages and heat it on the hob on medium. When hot, pour in the batter and transfer to the oven to bake for 30–35 minutes until golden.

3 For the gravy, heat the frying pan containing the leftover oil. Add the wine and bubble on a medium heat, scraping up any bits from the base of the pan. Reduce the heat, mix the cornflour with a little water to form a paste, and add to the pan, stirring constantly. Gradually pour in the stock, season to taste, and add the rosemary. Bring to the boil, then simmer, stirring, for 10 minutes. Season to taste. Strain to remove any lumps and the rosemary, pour into a jug, and serve with the toad in the hole.

serves 4

prep 15 mins
• cook 45 mins

GUIDELINES per serving

●●○ calories

●●● saturated fat

●●● salt

Blackberry and apple pie

A classic pie using late summer fruits. Omit the spices and serve with gluten-free ice cream to make this perfect for kids.

INGREDIENTS

450g (1lb) gluten-free
  shortcrust pastry (see p10)
gluten-free plain flour, for dusting
1 egg, lightly beaten
1 tbsp caster sugar

For the filling

3 cooking apples, peeled,
  cored, and sliced

1 star anise
1 vanilla pod, split lengthways
pinch of freshly grated nutmeg
100g (3½oz) demerara sugar
250g (9oz) blackberries
zest of ½ lemon or ½ orange

METHOD

1 Set aside one-third of the pastry for the lid. On a lightly floured surface, roll out the remaining pastry into a circle large enough to line the pie dish and overlap the sides. Chill in the fridge while you prepare the filling.

2 Place the apple in a pan with 6 tablespoons cold water, add the star anise, vanilla pod, nutmeg, and half the sugar, and cook over a gentle heat for 10–15 minutes until the apples begin to soften. Set aside for 20 minutes to allow the flavours to infuse.

3 Sprinkle the pastry base with the remaining sugar. Remove the vanilla pod, star anise, and any excess liquid from the apples. Arrange the apple slices over the pastry, then add the blackberries and lemon or orange zest.

4 Wet the edges of the pastry with a little water. Roll out the pastry for the lid and drape, pressing the edges to seal. Trim the edges and slash the top a couple of times. Brush with half the egg and chill for 20 minutes.

5 Preheat the oven to 200°C (400°F/Gas 6). Brush the pie with the remaining egg and sprinkle with caster sugar. Bake for 40–50 minutes until golden. If it starts to brown too much, cover the top with foil. Leave to cool slightly and serve warm.

serves 6

prep 15 mins
plus chilling
• cook 40-45 mins

18cm (7in)
round pie dish

3 months

GUIDELINES per serving
●●● calories
●●○ saturated fat
●○○ salt

Passion fruit and lemon soufflés

This is a really easy version of a sweet soufflé that relies on good-quality lemon curd.

INGREDIENTS

30g (1oz) unsalted butter, melted
115g (4oz) caster sugar, plus
  6 tsp for sprinkling
4 passion fruit
4 tbsp gluten-free lemon curd
4 eggs, separated
icing sugar, for sprinkling

METHOD

1 Preheat the oven to 200°C (400°F/Gas 6). Grease the ramekin dishes generously with the butter, then dust each with 1 teaspoon caster sugar. Put them in the fridge while you prepare the soufflé mixture.

2 Scoop seeds from the passion fruit and strain through a nylon sieve set over a bowl, to collect the juice. Discard pips and stir juice into the lemon curd along with the egg yolks.

3 Whisk the egg whites in a grease-free bowl using an electric whisk until stiff peaks form. Add the caster sugar and whisk until the mixture is stiff and shiny. Stir a heaped tablespoonful of the egg whites into the curd mixture to loosen it. Gently fold remaining egg whites into the mixture; do this slowly and gently so you don't knock out the air.

4 Divide the mixture between the ramekins, tap them on the work surface so that the mixture settles inside, then wipe a clean finger around the inside edge of each dish; this helps the soufflés rise evenly. Bake for 12–15 minutes or until well-risen and golden. Remove from the oven, transfer each ramekin to a plate, and sprinkle with icing sugar before serving.

 serves 6

 prep 15 mins
• cook 12-15 mins

 6 x 150ml (5fl oz) ramekin dishes

Lemon tart

Take care to ensure there are no holes in the pastry case or all that delicious lemon cream filling may leak out.

INGREDIENTS
400g (14oz) gluten-free
  shortcrust pastry (see p10)
gluten-free plain flour, for dusting
icing sugar, for dusting

For the filling
5 eggs
200g (7oz) caster sugar
250ml (9fl oz) double cream
125ml (4fl oz) lemon juice
  and grated zest of 4 lemons

METHOD
1 Preheat the oven to 200°C (400°F/Gas 6). Roll out the pastry on a lightly floured surface to a thickness of 5mm (¼in). Line the tin with the pastry, patching up any holes. Trim any surplus and neaten. Prick the base with a fork. Line with baking parchment and fill with baking beans, and bake in the oven for 15 minutes. Remove the beans and paper, and return to the oven for 5 minutes to crisp up. Set aside to cool.
2 While the tart is baking, prepare the filling. Place the eggs in a bowl and whisk gently. Add the sugar and mix well, then pour in the cream and the lemon juice and stir. Strain the mixture through a nylon sieve so it is smooth, then stir through the lemon zest. Reduce the oven temperature to 150°C (300°F/Gas 2).
3 Sit the tin on a baking sheet, then carefully pour the lemon mixture into the pastry case to fill. You can put it in the oven, pull out the shelf a little, and top up to save any spills. Bake in the oven for 50 minutes or until the filling is just starting to set; it will continue to set once out of the oven. Remove and leave to cool completely. To serve, dust with icing sugar.

serves 8

prep 30 mins
• cook 1 hour 10 mins

20.5cml (8in) round
loose-bottomed tart tin

GUIDELINES per serving
calories
saturated fat
salt

Chocolate and date sponge puddings

A hard-to-beat warming winter pudding served with a creamy chocolate sauce.

INGREDIENTS

250g (9oz) block of dried dates, stoned and chopped
1 tsp gluten-free bicarbonate of soda
145g (5oz) unsalted butter, softened, plus extra for greasing
280g (9½oz) light muscovado sugar
2 tbsp golden syrup
3 eggs

140g (5oz) gluten-free self-raising flour
60g (2oz) cocoa powder
90ml (3fl oz) milk
200ml (7fl oz) double cream
60g (2oz) dark chocolate (70% cocoa solids)

METHOD

1 Preheat the oven to 160°C (325°F/Gas 3). Put the dates in a pan with 175ml (6fl oz) water and bring to the boil. Remove from the heat, add the soda, stir, and set aside to cool. Grease and line the moulds with baking parchment. Place 85g (3oz) butter, 140g (5oz) sugar, and the syrup in a large bowl and whisk until creamy. Add the eggs gradually, whisking between additions. Add the flour, cocoa powder, and milk, and whisk again. Stir in the date mixture.

2 Divide the mixture between the prepared moulds. Cover each with a square of baking parchment and foil, pleated in the middle to allow the puddings to rise. Tightly pinch around the edges to form a good seal. Stand them in a roasting tin and pour boiling water to halfway up the outside of the moulds. Bake for 35–40 minutes or until the sponges are risen and firm to the touch. Remove from the oven and set aside.

3 For the sauce, place remaining sugar and butter, and half the cream in a small pan and bring to the boil, stirring until the sugar dissolves. Bubble for 1 minute. Remove from heat and add the remaining cream and the chocolate, stirring until the sauce is smooth.

4 Invert puddings onto serving plates, remove lining papers, and spoon over the sauce.

serves 6

prep 20 mins
• cook 35-40 mins

6 x 175ml (6fl oz) dariole moulds or ramekins

GUIDELINES per serving
calories
saturated fat
salt

White chocolate and raspberry muffins

A perfect balance of sweet white chocolate and tart raspberries makes these muffins hard to resist!

INGREDIENTS

300g (10oz) gluten-free plain flour
1½ tsp gluten-free baking powder
1 tsp xanthan gum
pinch of salt
175g (6oz) caster sugar
2 eggs
100g (3½oz) butter, melted
200ml (7fl oz) milk
175g (6oz) raspberries
140g (5oz) white chocolate, chopped

METHOD

1 Preheat the oven to 200°C (400°F/Gas 6). Sift the flour, baking powder, xanthan, salt, and sugar into a large bowl.

2 In another bowl, mix the eggs, butter, and milk, then pour into the dry ingredients along with the raspberries and 115g (4oz) chocolate. Mix briefly until just combined. Don't over-mix: it should still be a little lumpy.

3 Divide the mixture between the paper cases so they are two-thirds full. Bake in the oven for 25–30 minutes or until the centres spring back when lightly touched. Cool in the trays for 5 minutes before transferring to a wire rack. To finish, melt the remaining chocolate in a small heatproof bowl set over a pan of gently simmering water. Spoon the melted chocolate into the paper icing bag, snip off the tip of the bag, and drizzle the melted chocolate over the cakes in a zigzag pattern. Leave to set.

serves 16

prep 15 mins
plus cooling
• cook 25-30 mins

2 x deep, 12-hole muffin tray lined with 16 paper cases, and a greasproof paper icing bag

2 months

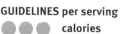
GUIDELINES per serving
●●● calories
●●● saturated fat
●●○ salt

London, New York, Melbourne, Munich, and Delhi

Written by Heather Whinney, Jane Lawrie & Fiona Hunter

Editors Cecile Landau, Alastair Laing, Chitra Subramanyam

Designers Katherine Raj, Prashant Kumar, Anamica Roy

Jacket Designer Mark Penfound

DTP Designer Kavita Varma

Photography William Shaw

Senior Producer Pieta Pemberton

Important Every effort has been made to ensure that the information contained in this book is complete and accurate. However, neither the publisher nor the authors are engaged in rendering professional advice or services to the individual reader. Professional medical advice should be obtained on personal health matters. Neither the publisher nor the authors accept any legal responsibility for any personal injury or other damage or loss arising from the use or misuse of the information and advice in this book.

First published in Great Britain in 2013
Material in this publication was previously published in *The Gluten-Free Cookbook* (2012) by Dorling Kindersley Limited
80 Strand, London WC2R 0RL
Penguin Group (UK)

10 9 8 7 6 5 4 3 2 1
001-192536-Feb/13

A CIP catalogue record for this book is available from the British Library.

ISBN 978-1-4093-2600-7

Printed and bound in China by Hung Hing Printing Co. Ltd.